# THE SECRET LIFE OF COWS
## GLEN WEXLER

❧

FOREWORD BY ERIC IDLE

**Andrews McMeel
Publishing, LLC**
Kansas City

WHEN YOU SEE COWS STANDING IN A PASTURE BLANDLY CHEWING SOME DREARY BIT OF GRASS AND STARING INTO THE MIDDLE DISTANCE, YOU'D NEVER GUESS WHAT LIES BENEATH THAT PLACID EXTERIOR.

WE ONLY SEE THEM AS WE DO BECAUSE THEY'RE TRAINED TO HIDE THEIR "ALTERNATIVE" LIFESTYLE. THEY'RE THE LIBRARIANS OF THE ANIMAL WORLD; MILD BY DAY, WILD BY NIGHT.

# WELCOME TO THE SECRET LIFE OF COWS . . .

A VIBRANT COUNTERCULTURE WHERE THE DIVINE BOVINE MAKE THEIR INNERMOST FANTASIES COME TRUE. ↩

# CIAO COW

As everybody knows I probably know more about cows than anyone on this planet. Actually that's not true. It's a bald-faced lie. (Why *bald-faced* incidentally, don't bearded people lie just as well? Surely they lie better because you can't see their faces?) Sorry, I digress.

The thing is, I'm a bit stumped. This Glen Wexler person called me up and asked me to write a foreword for his book and frankly I don't know a single thing about him, about photography, or for that matter about cows. So I'm kind of stuck out on a limb here, *busking* as we call it, faking it, as my wife calls it, or telling the truth to the American people as your politicians put it.

So what do I do? Do I come clean and leave the rest of the page empty? Do I bullshit for a bit? (Incidentally *there's* a cow reference right there.) Or do I try and pretend that my

esoteric knowledge of cows in comedy somehow qualifies me to waste your time like this? Because I do know a bit about cows in comedy. Here's what I know:
**Cows are always funny.**

There is a cow in the movie *Monty Python and the Holy Grail*. It is thrown over the battlements and squashes a page. "Fetchez la vache," says the French Taunter, and the French knights appear with a cow which they load on to a trebuchet (which is French for a machine that chucks cows).

We do the same scene in *Spamalot,* on Broadway. We throw a cow over the battlements – it lands on Patsy, Arthur's page, every night. And most matinées. (Occasionally they miss.) We even had a cow song. We thought it would be funny if we gave the cow a sad and touching farewell song as she went off to war. It wasn't.

COW:

> I'm just a lonely cow who has a dream
> That each and every one of us is part
> of nature's scheme
> That somehow every single cow
> Can make a difference to just how
> This world is now today – it's true
> So here's my final moo!

It was just too sad. You can't have an elegant Christian Dior cow singing a heartbreaking farewell and then being thrown over the battlements and expect to get a laugh. We now care about the damn cow. So here's what I learned:
**Cows aren't always funny.**

So it got cut in Chicago. Not the first cow that got cut in Chicago, which is practically the center of the cow cutting world. They even have a "Hamburger U" there, which shows just how weird and strange they are.

So, let me see, cows . . . ah, yes. In Bavaria once with Monty Python we filmed the Bad Toltz Cattle Herd giving a performance of *The Merchant of Venice*. We shot lots of cows in Shakespearian costume wandering around the field with Shakespearian subtitles and lots of mooing.

"What news on the Rialto Antonio?"

I played a very sincere German theatre critic: "*The Merchant of Venice* is a very difficult play for cows . . ."

Here's what I learned:

**Sometimes cows aren't even funny in German.**

So now what have I got? Well, frankly, nothing. I have some chicken stories. An odd tale about a duck. *What?* Say something about Glen? Well, OK. Glen is a seven-foot Scotsman with a wooden leg whom I met Frog Rolling on an Eskimo trip in Northern Greenland. We were sheltering in a sauna at a local bordello with an Icelandic babe called Splut . . . no, I agree, it's a hopeless and pathetic lie. You see I haven't even met him. It's useless. I'm dismal as a foreword writer. I've got nothing to say. I didn't want this job, I didn't ask for this job. I just wanted to be . . . a lumberjack!

So why did I do it? Why did I take it on? Well, honestly, I did it for the money. The publishers came to me and said, "Eric we will give you thirty thousand pounds if you will write a foreword . . ." What? They offered how much? Nothing? Jeeze. Well that's it then. I'm out of here. Let's face it, if you don't find these pictures funny on first sight no amount of forewords will persuade you otherwise. So, frankly, enjoy.

ERIC IDLE

**Bibliography**
*The Cow Through the Ages*
*The Seven Ages of Spam*
*Why the Cow Almost Became the Symbol of America?*
*The Cow in Literature With Regard to Jane Austen and Dickens*
*Fetchez La Vache – A French Dairy Dictionary*

French knights prepare to launch a cow from a trebuchet over a castle wall at the unsuspecting Englishmen. From a certain perspective bystanders observed, "the cow jumped over the moon."

# CHAPTER ONE
## SUPERHERO COWS

THE DAY WILL COME WHEN . . .

THE COW WILL HAVE USE FOR HER TAIL.

Irish Proverb ⁓

PLATE I

15

PLATE II

PLATE III

PLATE IV

THE COW IS OF THE BOVINE ILK;

ONE END IS MOO, THE OTHER, MILK.

Ogden Nash

PLATE V

PLATE VI

PLATE VII

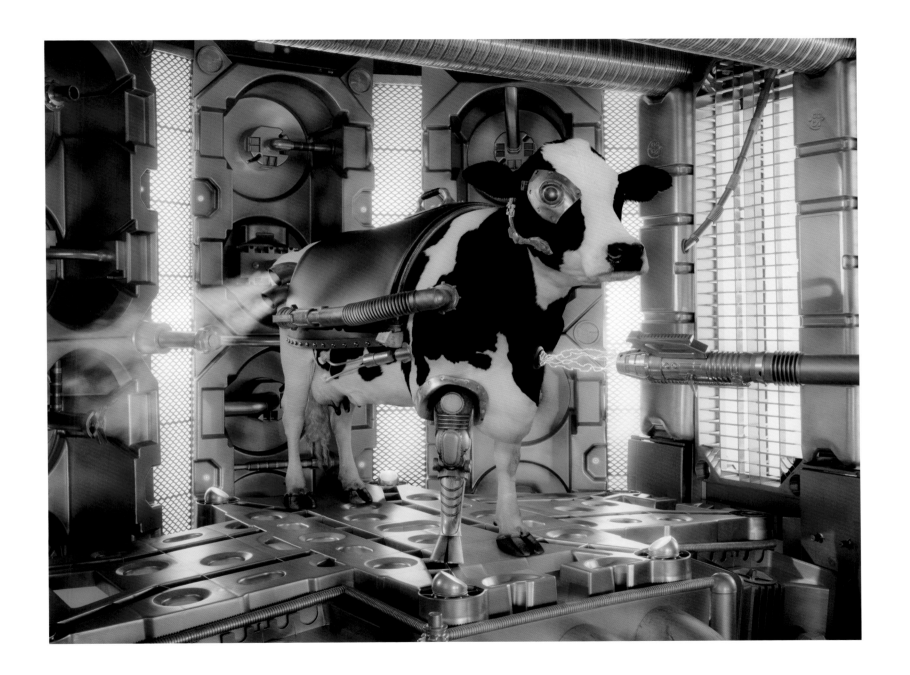

PLATE VIII

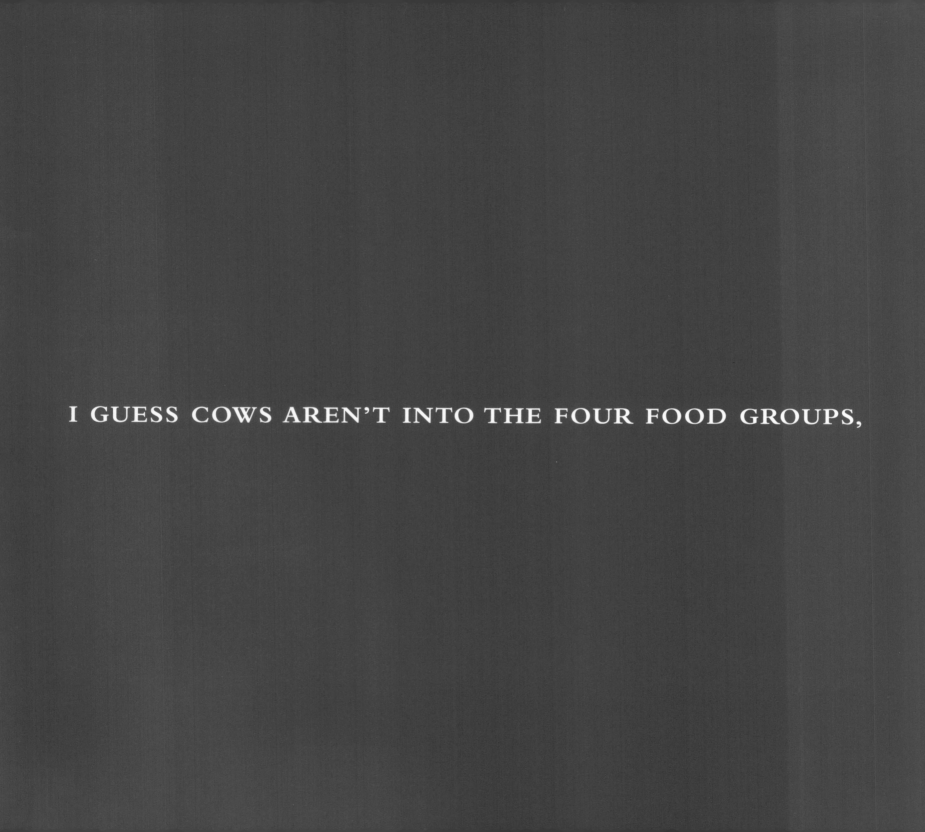

I GUESS COWS AREN'T INTO THE FOUR FOOD GROUPS,

ESPECIALLY WHEN *THEY* ARE TWO OF THEM.

Anthony Clark ✌

PLATE IX

PLATE X

PLATE XI

PLATE XII

# CHAPTER TWO
# SECRET AGENT COWS

COW . . .

. . . ABUNGA!

PLATE XIII

PLATE XIV

PLATE XV

PLATE XVI

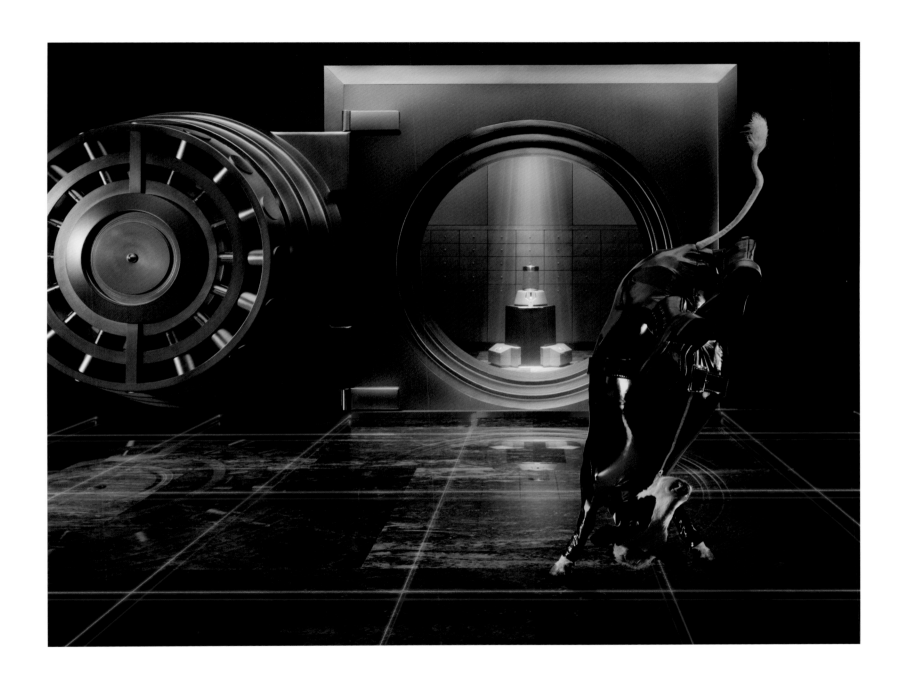

SCIENTISTS TELL US THAT THE FASTEST ANIMAL
ON EARTH, WITH A TOP SPEED OF . . .

120 FEET PER SECOND, IS A COW THAT HAS BEEN DROPPED OUT OF A HELICOPTER.

Dave Barry ⟿

PLATE XVII

PLATE XVIII

PLATE XIX

PLATE XX

LOOK AT THOSE COWS AND REMEMBER THAT
THE GREATEST SCIENTISTS . . .

HAVE NEVER DISCOVERED HOW TO TURN
GRASS INTO MILK.

Michael Pupin ⮎⮌

PLATE XXI

PLATE XXII

PLATE XXIII

PLATE XXIV

# PLATES

**DIVINE BOVINE**
COVER

**DISEMBARKING COWS**
PAGE 2 – 3

**PREFLIGHT**
PAGE 9

**SUPERHERO COWS**
PAGE 10

### THE SWATTER
PLATE I, PAGE 15

### KOWRATÉ
PLATE II, PAGE 17

### GRISTLE MISSILE
PLATE III, PAGE 19

### DECIBELL
PLATE IV, PAGE 21

2%

PLATE V, PAGE 25

LEATHERNECK

PLATE VI, PAGE 27

COWBORG

PLATE VII, PAGE 29

UNTIPPABLE

PLATE VIII, PAGE 31

## COWMELEON

PLATE IX, PAGE 35

## HOLSTOY

PLATE X, PAGE 37

## COLD CUT

PLATE XI, PAGE 39

## LITTLE BIG HOOF

PLATE XII, PAGE 41

## SECRET AGENT COWS
PAGE 42

## MR. T-BONE
PLATE XIII, PAGE 47

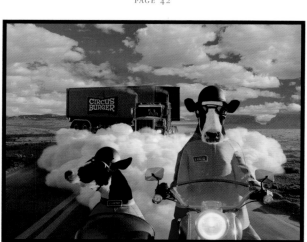

## HELMÜT HOLSTEIN
PLATE XIV, PAGE 49

## FILIPPE MIGNON
PLATE XV, PAGE 51

### VIENNA SAUCY
PLATE XVI, PAGE 53

### ANGUS BLACK & HONEY DIJON
PLATE XVII, PAGE 57

### SIR LOIN
PLATE XVIII, PAGE 59

### MOO JIT SU
PLATE XIX, PAGE 61

**BIFF STROGANOFF**

PLATE XX, PAGE 63

**ABACUS BOUILLON**

PLATE XXI, PAGE 67

**MAX SUEDE**

PLATE XXII, PAGE 69

**MOO RYKER**

PLATE XXIII, PAGE 71

AGENT M₂00
PLATE XXIV, PAGE 73

WANDERING COW
PAGE 92

The Superhero Cows and Secret Agent Cows originally appeared in the 2004 or 2005 Chick-fil-A® Cow Calendars.
The cow character names are used with the permission of Chick-fil-A, Inc.

Production credits: set design, props, and miniatures: Anthony Tremblay; first photo assistant: Ubaldo Holguin; second photo assistant: Roy Yoshioka; digital imaging artists for Glen Wexler Studio: Carsten Steinhausen, Carolyn Winslow and Czarina Buckingham; wardrobe stylist: Lori "Tin" Wornom; make-up and hair (Splut): Mitzi Spallas/Cloutier; grooming: Anne Marso; costume fabrication: James Hayes, Gayle Davis and Denise Brassard; model makers: Carl Horner, Wyatt Weed, Tim Whidden, Jim Arbaugh, Frank Dietz, Erik Stohl, and Jason Garner; cow sculpture: Charles Rivera; miniature cow castings: Merritt Productions; cow photography producer: Mark Gomez/Firedog Productions; cows and wranglers: Worldwide Movie Rentals; pyrotechnics: Joe Viskocil; seamstress: Rosaria Vitale; principal talent: Lyndall Jarvis/Next Model Management (Splut) and Jordi Caballero/CESD Talent (card dealer).

# WHAT'S FOR LUNCH?

I love my job . . . most of the time. People pay me to have a tremendous amount of fun, and to create images that would be prohibitively expensive without a well-funded commission.

I have been given the opportunity to photograph the very famous, create some well-known album covers, and am often entrusted with the realization of multi-million-dollar advertising campaigns. The best part is that I am allowed to make images that I love to create. Not that it isn't a lot of hard work and long hours. It is an amazing process when you and a crew of up to 15 or 20 all collaborate towards a singular vision. The scope of production is very much like making a film, but all of this effort is fixed on a single frame. With a project that aims for the ridiculous, as with the cows, it's great to be on a set all day where everyone can't help but smile.

The "Superheroes" and "Secret Agents" were commissioned by Chick-fil-A, a fast-food restaurant that sells chicken sandwiches primarily in the southern and southeastern regions of the United States.

Chick-fil-A's advertising agency, The Richards Group, markets the sandwiches by using cow characters to advocate the consumption of chicken instead of hamburgers. Much of the work in this book was originally used for their 2004 and 2005 theme-based calendars. I was awarded the assignments based on my assumed expertise in photographing cows, a unique specialty among advertising photographers (and a double-edged sword because, in the specialty obsessed commercial market, some now confuse my standing as an agricultural photographer).

What I actually do is create photo-illustrations of manufactured or altered realities. My work relies on the perceived (but waning) credibility inherent in the photographic image. I recombine elements of the real world to create a fantastical vision in which the components often react in a surreal or absurd manner. This involves visualizing the finished image, then breaking down the plan for the final outcome into manageable components to be individually photographed and, finally, digitally seaming it all together. In order for this to work out successfully all compositional elements, lighting, and perspective decisions are carefully considered and determined prior to the shoot.

Prior to my coming on board, the advertising agency commissioned photographers to dress cows in costumes. This makes sense, sort of, but I dismissed the suggestion and approach in a nanosecond. The notion of getting cows to "perform" all dressed-up doesn't take into account that their bodily functions are both unpredictable and frequent, and that they are extremely poor at following direction – even the well-trained Hollywood cows used in commercials and films. I took a different approach.

My production designer and collaborator of nearly twenty years Anthony Tremblay enlisted the services of Charles Rivera to sculpt a very realistic one-third-size miniature cow. We next had a mould made from our sculpted cow for the purpose of creating several foam castings that could be cut and individually reassembled in the pose desired for each cow character. The cow forms were then appropriately dressed. The Superhero costumes were styled and fabricated by Gayle Davis. The Secret Agents were styled by Lori "Tin" Wornom, and the costumes fabricated by James Hayes, the same guy who creates wardrobe for the Muppets.

Anthony created production drawings for each set, and built them in miniature with a team of model makers. The one-third-scale sculpted cows were photographed in the miniature set environments. Both series required about 30 days each for principal set and element photography, followed by several days of photographing the actual cows. With the help and patience of a team of cow wranglers, the Hollywood cows were lit and shot in perspective to match their sculpted "body doubles" in the set photography. Special effects were also photographed, including an explosion that was created by Joe Viskocil, the pyrotechnic who blew up the Death Star in *Star Wars* and the White House in *Independence Day*. Following the two extensive photography productions, there were hundreds of elements to combine, requiring nearly six hundred hours total for post-production image editing.

In a recent interview for a fine art publication, the interviewer, unaware of the commercial context of the work asked me, "The series 'Bovine Superheroes' and 'Secret Agent Cows' have an ecological and ethical statement. Would you like to talk about this and about your beliefs?" The beauty of much of my commissioned work is that the images can often stand alone from the marketing purposes that set the parameters for their creation. The Superheroes and Secret Agents were created to sell fast-food chicken sandwiches. And it's funny that the cows are protecting their species by advocating that people eat chicken instead of them. But, after you take away the marketing copy, the viewer is forced to draw their own conclusions, which will perhaps lead to people examining issues bigger than "what's for lunch?" Or not.

In the end, the paradoxes surrounding art

and commerce, or the purpose and meaning of art, are better left to the art critics and scholars. There is no doubt that a personal point of view is embedded in the work, but, at the very least, we entertained ourselves during the creation of the images, and hopefully they will be enjoyed by many more.

In the foreword written for the catalogue of my recent retrospective, *25:25*, Tim Wride, the curator of photography of the Los Angeles County Museum of Art, writes,

*In a Stieglitz-perfect world, there was art photography, and then there was everything else. Nothing is quite so simple anymore, if indeed it was ever so even then. Today, commercial and editorial photographers stake claims in the fine art territory and, increasingly, recognized fine art photographers are allowing their images to be used within a commercial context. The simple fact is that the monolith that in the past we casually referred to as "the photographic market," has splintered into a dozen hybrid markets whose only boundaries are the shifting needs and tastes of those who create images and those who consume them. While perhaps approaching the tasks from diametrically opposed intentions, curators, and gallerists are constantly rediscovering images from an editorial or advertising past that are then subjected to the ritualized cleansing of an exhibition and reintroduced to polite society as art. It is not that the work itself has substantively changed, nor has its original intent been redefined; what has occurred over time is that certain images or bodies of work have begun to resonate differently to a different and often more sophisticated audience.*

So, there you have it.

I would like to acknowledge and thank the very talented agency art directors who hired me to create the images: Todd Tucker (Superheroes), Linsey Parks (Secret Agents) and Daniel Rodriguez (Disembarking Cows for Sony).

And thank you to Eric Idle, who I hope to meet someday.

**GLEN WEXLER**

COWBELL MOOSIC
HI-MOODELITY

STEROIDS

# MEAT THE BEEFLES!

## The First Album by England's Phenomenal Cow Combo

Cowbel
RECORDS

Glen Wexler photographed his first album cover for Quincy Jones Productions while still a student at Art Center College of Design. He quickly gained a reputation for his imaginative and elaborate photo illustrations for Michael Jackson, KISS, Van Halen, Rush, Black Sabbath, Yes, ZZ Top, and many others.

During the mid 1980s Glen's images began to attract advertising clients. His signature style has earned an international client base including Acura, Sony, Maxell, Adobe, Microsoft, Intel, Jeep, Toyota, Pfizer, Warner Bros. Pictures, and hundreds of others. Glen also creates feature photo illustrations for *Time* magazine.

Glen was among the original artists to adopt digital imaging technology as a tool in the creative process. Credited as a worldwide leader in the field, he has been invited to speak at the Seybold Conferences in New York and San Francisco, the PhotoPlus Expos in New York and Los Angeles, and at colleges across the United States.

Awards and recognition for Glen's images have been received from *Communication Arts, Graphis, Photo District News,* New York and Los Angeles Art Directors' Clubs, the Beldings, Icon Awards, International Photography Awards, NPPA, and Key Art Awards. Glen is profiled in *Communication Arts* (August 1999), French *Photo* (April 2001), *Creativity* (July 2005) and *Zoom* (February 2006).

In fall 2005, Wexler commemorated 25 years of his career with a gallery exhibition in Los Angeles and the release of his retrospective book *25:25*. Tim Wride, curator of photography for the Los Angeles County Museum of Art (LACMA), writes in the book's introduction, "Wexler's pictorial constancy as a risk taker and his deftness as a problem solver are the characteristics that distinguish his work and make his images both meaningful and memorable."

Glen resides in the Hollywood Hills with his wife and two children.

For more info visit www.glenwexler.com

Left: An early 1960s album cover project featuring an obscure, yet apparently influential, recording combo. The Beefles' unique cowbell compositions include "Twist and Moo," "I Want to Hold Your Tail," and "Love Me Moo." Unfortunately for the Beefles, the cowbell was overshadowed by the popularity of the electric guitar, an instrument they found physically challenging. It is interesting to note that a decade later the cowbell found its place in popular music with Blue Oyster Cult's rock classic "Don't Fear the Reaper." With a generation of young music fans chanting "MORE COWBELL!," it is quite possible we have not heard the last of the Beefles.

Eat Mor Chikin® is a registered trademark of CFA Properties, Inc.

This edition published in 2007 by Andrews McMeel Publishing, LLC,
an Andrews McMeel Universal company, 4520 Main Street, Kansas City, Missouri, 64111

First published in 2006 by PQ Blackwell Limited.

The publisher is grateful for literary permissions to reproduce those items subject to copyright. Every effort has been made to trace the copyright holders and the publisher apologizes for any unintentional omission. We would be pleased to hear from any not acknowledged here and undertake to make all reasonable efforts to include the appropriate acknowledgement in any subsequent editions. "*Scientists tell us that the fastest animal on earth, with a top speed of 120 feet per second, is a cow that has been dropped out of a helicopter.*" Used with permission of Dave Barry.

Design by Carolyn Lewis and Cameron Gibb
Additional text by Jim Hopkins

Printed by Midas Printing International Limted, China
ISBN-10: 0-7407-6311-3
ISBN-13: 978-0-7407-6311-3

www.andrewsmcmeel.com